For TRIS – love forever and always. W.R.

For Tilly and Charlie. T.J.

First published in 2026 by

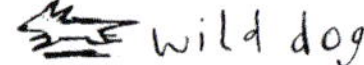

Melbourne, Australia
wdog.com.au

ISBN: 9781 742037 11 0

A catalogue record for this book is available from the National Library of Australia

Printed and bound in China by
Everbest Printing Investment Limited

10 9 8 7 6 5 4 3 2 1 26 27 28 29 30 31

FSC® is a non-profit international organisation established to promote the responsible management of the world's forests.

Wild Dog Books would like to thank the Fiona Wood Foundation for their endorsement of this book.

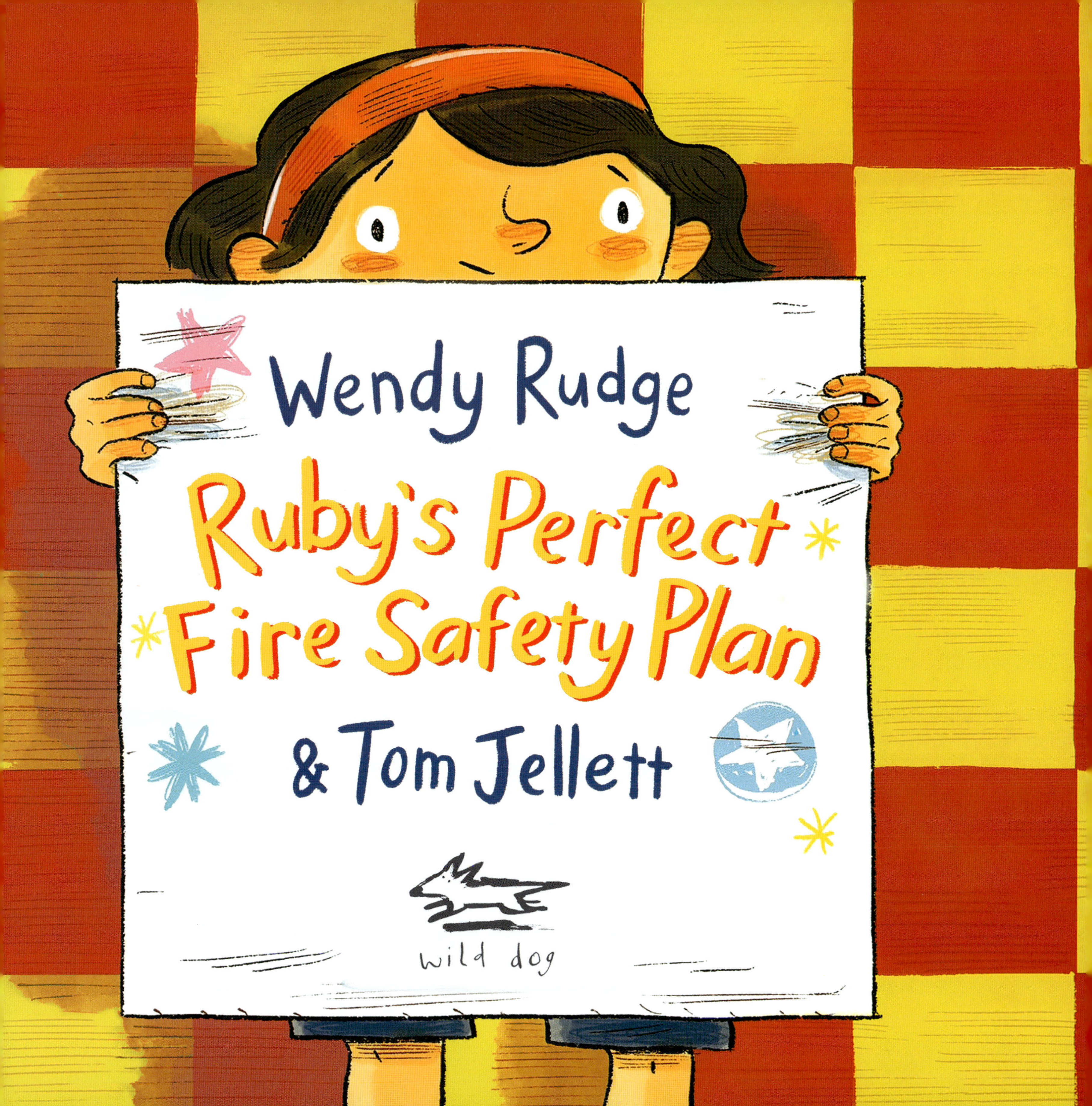
Wendy Rudge
Ruby's Perfect Fire Safety Plan
& Tom Jellett
wild dog

Ruby loved making plans. She had a plan for everything.

There was the plan for making the perfect sandwich,

the plan for organising the perfect sock drawer,

and the plan for holding the perfect birthday party was coming along nicely.

Today, Ruby was thinking about a different plan.

Firefighters from the local fire station had visited her class to talk about fire safety in the house.

Ruby didn't have a plan
for how to stay safe
in case of a fire.

Ruby called a family meeting.

'I know I'm not allowed to play with lighters and matches, but that's not the only way a fire starts,' she told Mum.

'Did you know there are many things in a house that can start a fire?' she asked Dad.

'We need to check for fire hazards in the house,' she explained to Gran.

Fire hazards
Ruby spots
1. Leaves overflowing in the guttering outside.
2. Double adapter being piggybacked on other powerpoints.
3. Curtains over an open window blowing near a candle.
Eleven

4. Phone charging under a pillow in a bedroom.
5. Socks drying on the heater.
6. Pot left unattended on the stovetop.

Ruby set about making a plan.

It was an important job and Ruby was determined to keep her family safe.

First, she drew a map of her whole house showing the safest ways to escape in case of a fire.

RUBY M

Then she made a poster with the emergency number for the Fire Brigade and her address with the three top tips in case of a fire.

FIRE BRIGADE 000
our address is 23 Green St
1. Don't take anything, just get down low and go, go, go!
2. Get out fast and stay out!
3. Wait for everybody at the family meeting spot by the letterbox
A

The next day Ruby called another family meeting to talk through her escape plan and how to fix the fire hazards she had spotted.

'But the plan's not quite finished. There's still more to do,' said Ruby. 'We need to check the smoke alarms. And not just once — *often*.'

'We also need to practise our fire escape plan regularly, just in case of a fire.'

'So now we need a fire drill.'

Ruby blew her whistle.

Mum, Dad and Gran jumped to their feet.

'What are you waiting for? Get down low and go, go, go!' Ruby said. 'Our family meeting spot is at the letterbox. And remember we stay together and call 000.'

Mum crawled expertly out under the imaginary smoke, Gran bumped her nose on the wall, and Dad got a bit tangled trying to stay low, but everyone got out of the house.

Ruby beamed with pride. 'Well done, family!'

'Great plan,' said Dad. 'I'm off to clean the gutters.'

'Brilliant,' said Mum. 'I'm off to mark dates for our fire drills on the calendar.'

'Best fire plan ever,' said Gran. 'I'm off to hang my socks on the clothesline.'

Ruby smiled proudly. 'The perfect plan for a fire safe family! Now, what to plan next?'

Fire Facts

Only call 000 in an emergency.

- Ask for the Fire Brigade and tell the operator your address.
- Always stay on the line until the operator tells you it's ok to hang up.

- Fire is hungry and needs three 'foods' to survive; heat, fuel and oxygen. Take away any one of these and the fire will go out!
- Remember to **stop, drop and roll** if your clothes catch on fire as it cuts off the air (oxygen) that feeds the flames and helps put out the fire.

- Working smoke alarms save lives during the day and at night. Your ability to smell is greatly reduced when you sleep. That is why a working smoke alarm is so important.

- Fire can move faster than you think – it can spread through a house very quickly. In just 30 seconds a small flame can become a big fire.

- **Get down low and go, go, go!**

Thick black smoke and poisonous gases rise towards the ceiling during a fire, so the safest air is closest to the floor. Crawl under smoke with your nose as low as possible.

• Draw up your Fire Escape Plan. Remember to include two exits for each room. Practise it with your family regularly.

• Once you're safely outside, never ever go back into a burning building for any reason. Firefighters have special equipment to rescue people and pets.

• Firefighters don't just fight fires. They also rescue people from car accidents, buildings and other dangerous situations.
They sometimes rescue trapped animals and assist in natural disasters.
They educate the public on fire safety, and they do lots of training.

• Firefighters' gear is super strong; a firefighter's helmet can withstand 4000 newtons of force. That's like having a small car pressing down on their head!
This helps keep firefighters safe when they're working.

• Fire trucks are very heavy; some fire trucks weigh as much as four elephants! They carry thousands of litres of water and lots of special equipment to fight fires and rescue people.

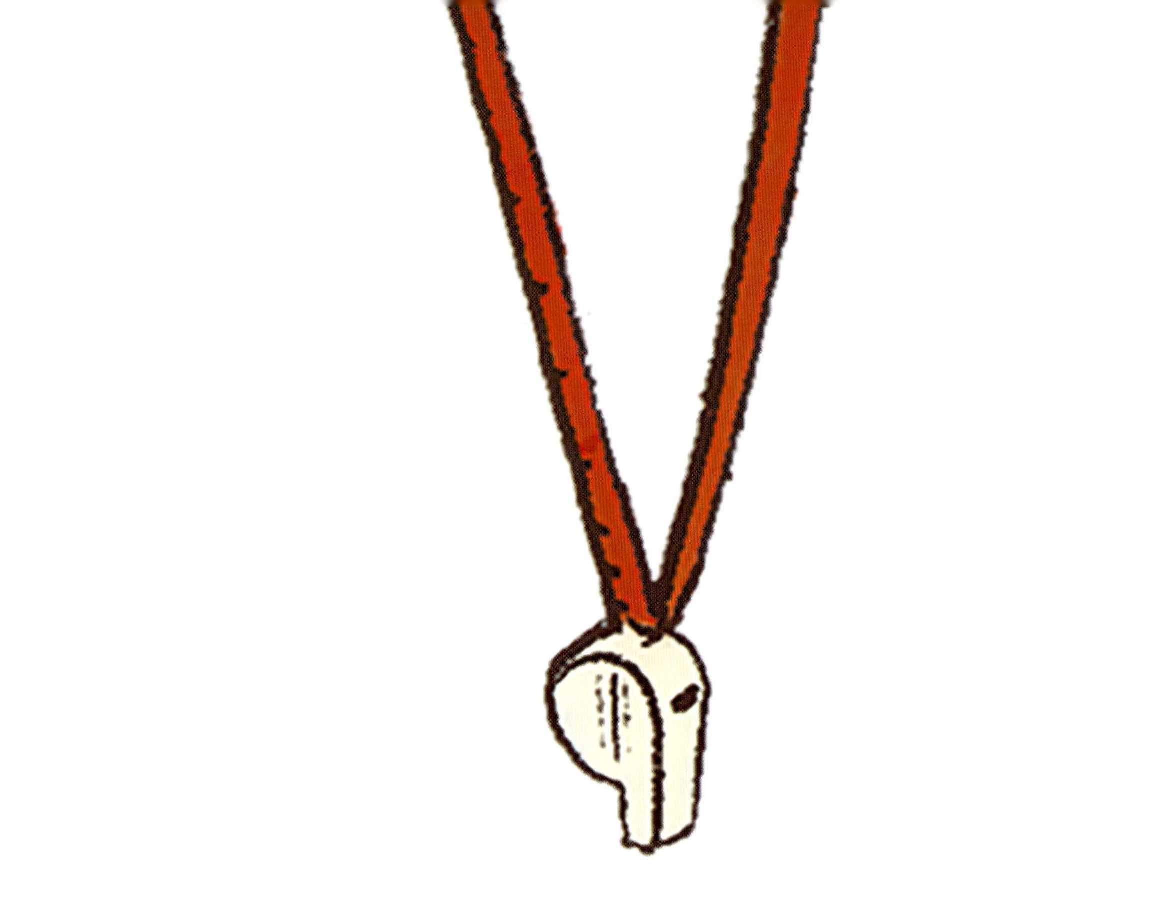